Origins

Buzz Off!

Damian Harvey ■ **Jonatronix**

OXFORD
UNIVERSITY PRESS

In this story

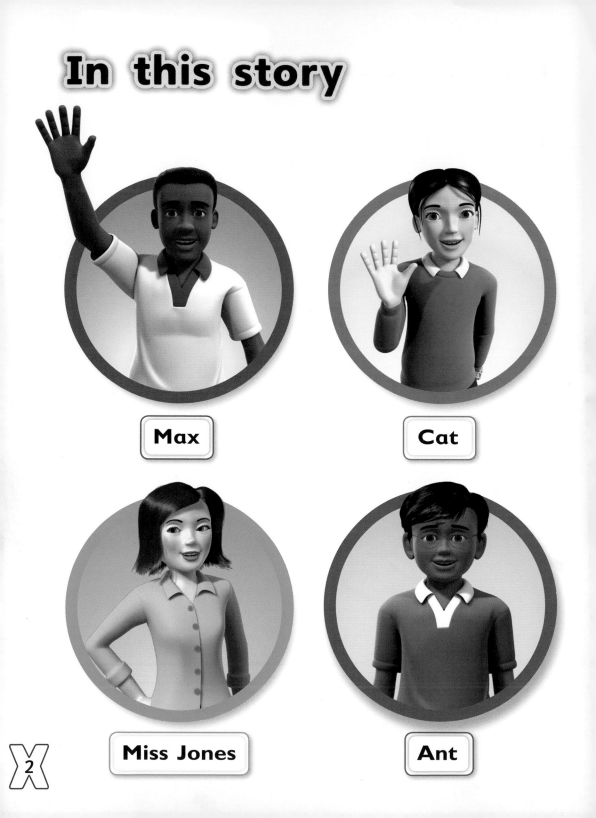

Max

Cat

Miss Jones

Ant

It was a hot day at the end of term. Miss Jones and the children were tidying the classroom.

Suddenly Cat gasped. She looked
at the floor.

"Look! Ants!" she said.

Then something buzzed past
Max's face.
"What was that?" asked Max.
"It's only a fly," said Miss Jones.
"It must have come through
the window."

The buzzing noise grew louder.
Soon they could see lots of flies.
They were buzzing around everywhere.
"Keep still. They will fly out of the
window soon," said Miss Jones.

Just then, the bell rang for lunch.
Everyone started to leave
the classroom.
"I will ask Mr Foster to get rid of
the bugs," said Miss Jones.

"Let's find out why the bugs have come in," Cat said.

"Good idea," said Max. "Look, there's Ant. He knows lots about bugs. He could help us."

Max and Cat told Ant about the
bugs. Ant watched them.

"All of the ants are going the same way. They are going into the cupboard. Let's follow them!" said Ant.

The children pushed the buttons on their watches.

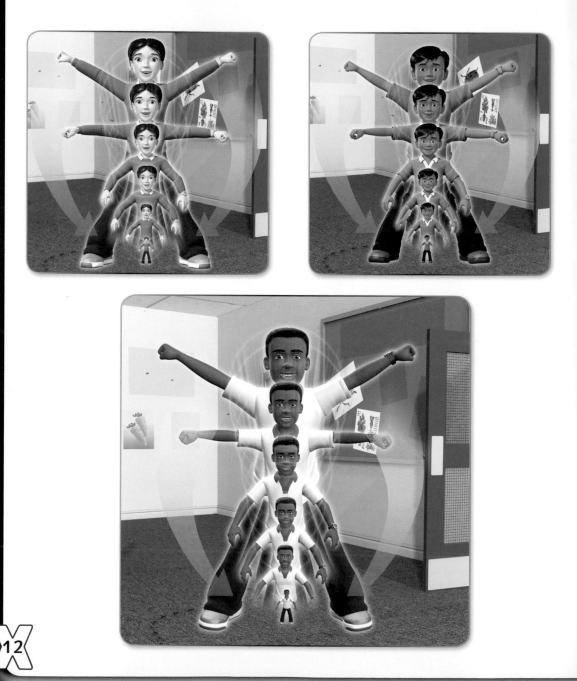

They followed the bugs.
"What's that?" asked Ant.
"It's our healthy teeth poster," said
Cat. "We have just taken it off
the wall."

What's that?

Keep Your Good Foods

Teeth Healthy

Bad Foods

Ant pointed at the sweets.
"Ants and flies like sweet things!"
he said. "That's why they are
coming in here."

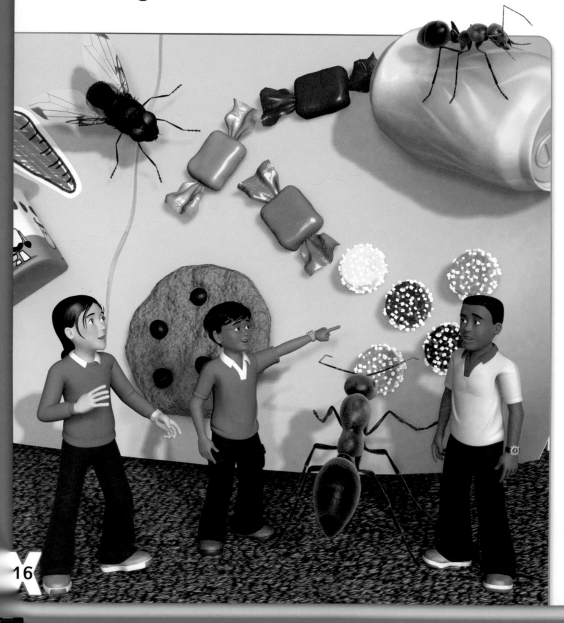

"They cannot stay in our classroom! We need to get them outside," said Cat.
Max had an idea.

"We could lead them outside
with the sweets," said Max.
"They will follow us!"

Cat picked up a sweet. Max and Ant rolled the can.

The ants followed them. The flies followed them. The wasps followed them. Max, Cat and Ant went into the playground. No one saw them.

They got to the bin. They pushed the buttons on their watches.

They put the sweet things in the bin.

The bell rang. Max and Cat went back to class. Mr Foster was talking to Miss Jones.

Find out more

Read about an alien invasion in ...

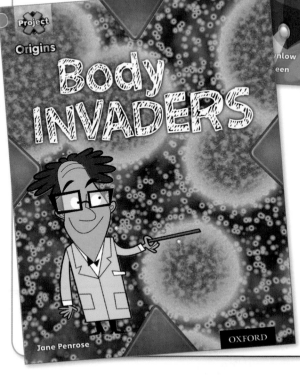

... and find out how germs invade the body.